You're Totally Awesome!

What Kids are saying about
You're Totally Awesome!
The **POWER** of Acknowledgment for Kids

"The book is made of many good stories where characters use the power of acknowledgment.

It really got me thinking how I could change my behavior to make others feel better. The book was easy to read and made me feel happy. I liked the 2nd chapter the most. **Which one will you like the most?**"

— Max Kokko, age 11, Vantaa, in southern Finland
(Max likes sports. He plays football, speed skates and he also plays piano. At school he likes mathematics in addition to sports.)

"After reading this book, I realized a compliment would make someone very happy. I think this book will inspire kids to acknowledge the things people are good at."

— Julia Match, age 11, Long Island, New York
(Julia plays the viola and she studies Jiu Jitsu.)

"This book was really fun and enjoyable to read. I learned all about acknowledgment and putting it into practice, so now I can acknowledge my friends and just as important, my parents."

— Hanna Pattrick, age 8
(Hanna lives in Vantaa, in southern Finland. She has a Finnish mom and an English dad. Her hobbies include crafting, ice skating and gym.)

"I don't think bullies understand how they affect others. Reading this book would help everyone understand that it's better to acknowledge others rather then put them down!**"**

— **Bodie Porter**, age 13, Monett, Missouri
(Bodie loves building custom Lego transformers, mastering challenging games and kayaking in the summer.)

"The book *You're Totally Awesome!* is a good read for pre-teens and teens, whether they want to better themselves or parents want to teach the child about being responsible for another's feelings with their actions. The book teaches kids and teens to pay it forward, look for ways to help when you think you can, without crossing the boundaries of someone's business, and to help others you help feel like they should pay it forward, too. It carries a sweet message about caring for others and I think others really should read it. It could help our future become better.**"**

— **Lauren Degnan**, age 16, Poughkeepsie, New York
(Lauren enjoys music, to play and to listen to; she loves writing short stories, and hanging out with her friends and acting like they are five.)

"These stories can help kids in so many situations! Being a person with type 1 diabetes, I thought that the chapter on being diagnosed with diabetes accurately showed many feelings that kids with diabetes experience, especially right after diagnosis. I hope that the message in this story inspires kids to prioritize their health.**"**

— **Analeigh Hughes**, age 15, Rockland County, New York
(Analeigh has had diabetes for 10 years and doesn't let it stop her! She is a competitive swimmer on three teams, studies voice and loves music and reading.)

"I thought this book was amazing and a great learning experience. This book made me realize how I need to acknowledge the people in my life, especially my amazing, wonderful, perfect girlfriend."

— RJ Elite, age 13, Staten Island, New York
(RJ loves football, both playing and rooting for the New York Giants, playing games on XBox, & watching TV series.)

"I think the stories in this book are really good and it was a better decision to use real people's stories instead of stories that you could just make up that no one could relate to. Before I read this book, I didn't really notice how much the power of acknowledgment can change one person. Now that I have read this book, I will do my best to acknowledge my friends in everything I do. Whether it be in school, after school activities, or just hanging out with friends, I will acknowledge everyone I can including my parents, teachers and coaches."

— Vanessa Tamarit, age 11, North Bergen, New Jersey
(Vanessa loves helping younger children, singing, tap dancing, ballet dancing, acting, baseball, basketball, and most of all hanging out with friends.)

What Grown-ups are saying about
You're Totally Awesome!
The **POWER** of Acknowledgment for Kids

"*You're Totally Awesome* provides an honest, uplifting, genuine approach for making the world a better place. Teaching children to acknowledge others will result in more positive interactions at school, on the playground, and at the dinner table! As a school principal and mother, I understand, first hand, the power of acknowledging others, and also of being acknowledged for the work I do. Judy's book is a great teaching tool — I especially appreciate the activities at the end of each chapter which allow time and space for reflection. I imagine my students making meaningful connections with the characters in the book fostering an atmosphere of respect and confidence, leading to greater learning and understanding."

> — **Cheryl Hopper,** *Principal*
> Edgemont Montessori School, Montclair, NJ

"I really like this book, because it asks the kids to think and not just read. The questions/writing at the end of each section allows the child to think about the concept as it relates to him or her. I believe this helps to internalize the message in a way that just reading doesn't. Children are naturally self-centered — they hopefully become less so as they get older. But that doesn't mean they can't be coached by an adult (or this book) to help them gain empathy. It's a wonderful book!"

> —**Elaine Bohner,** *mother of three, a boy and a girl ages 10 and 4, who go to Cornerstone Elementary School, Rancho Palos Verdes, California and a daughter, age 26*

"On my second deployment to the Middle East, I had the privilege of reading the manuscript for this book. I loved it so much I did a video reading of the "Cupcake for Hector" story and sent it to my children. Three years later, the cupcake story still comes up in conversation. It's simply amazing! Judy has an amazing gift; she brings out the sunshine and shows people how to tap into their inner energy to make the world a brighter place. What's amazing about this collection of stories is children don't need to be taught how to live in the moment and make a difference, they just know how to do it. Hector's story is the most amazing example of how a child, living and acknowledging the moment, is able to heal an undefined hole in a gentleman's heart. This book is a great tool for anyone looking to re-learn the childhood secret of enjoying and living in the moment, while helping children learn how to make acknowledgment an important part of their lives. "

— Shana Serrano, *Process Coordinator*,
Department of the Army Civilian (DAC), USAFRICOM

"Judy Umlas has successfully and creatively expanded her message of acknowledgment to the language of children. With her most recent work, *You're Totally Awesome! The Power of Acknowledgment for Kids*, Judy has skillfully transferred her higher consciousness thinking of taking others' gifts, talents and feelings into consideration and translated this into the voice of reason for both children and adults. She clearly explains how this shift in thinking can create "miracles."

This work is essential for all of us who are involved with children: parents, grandparents, teachers, bus drivers, coaches, nannies, family therapists, etc. Ms. Umlas remains consistent in her message that when we can get beyond our own egos and can instead focus on the positive in others, everyone benefits and grows. "

— **Steve A. Roithmayr, MSW, PhD, Family Therapist**

"As a family therapist and relationship coach for over 30 years, the one missing ingredient in most of the relationships which have been in conflict and crisis is that of acknowledgment. This new book by Judy Umlas for children — and in alliance with children — is a brilliant and essential tool which can provide an important ingredient for children to use in their relationships, going through life. It is a tool I wish I had been able to give parents many years ago; it is a teaching tool for the entire family. It's the old story: in order to learn something effectively, TEACH it! When the whole family sits down with this book, reviews each principle, shares each story, and then works through the "questions for kids" section at the conclusion of each chapter, not only do the children have the wisdom and practical tools for navigating relationships in their own lives in school and beyond, but the parents have the tools for their own use and application as well. Sometimes the parents learn the most valuable lessons when the little child leads them. Thank you Judy for this AMAZING gift!"

> — **Sheila Pearl, M.S.W.**, *Educator, Family Therapist,*
> *Relationship Coach, Co-author in **"Pearls of Wisdom:***
> ***30 Inspirational Ideas for Living Your Best Life"***

"My son unfortunately is a victim of bullying at school. While we have had many discussions with the principal at the schools he has attended over the years, nothing really seems to help the situation. My son and I found great value in the message of kindness and the importance of acknowledgment and believe that if Judy's book was in the hands of his classmates maybe the message would come across to those who bully. I will be sharing Judy's book with the principal at my son's school and suggest that the teachers and/or school as a whole incorporate the book with its profound message to the ongoing efforts to stamp out the bullying ways of kids that have not been shown a better way."

> — **Wendy Shields**, *A Concerned Mother*

"I love the book! My initial thought is a desire to work this into our Yellow Ribbon Week* celebrations, complement our Rachel's Challenge program with this, and have it resonate with every elementary school child possible, so that they can grow into adults who understand the power of acknowledgment and how just one small act, or lack thereof, can cause a dramatic shift in the reality of someone's world.

The book was a well-written, easy to understand kids' book, full of examples children can visualize along with their parents. It goes further than telling kids to "be nice" — it sets the stage for HOW children can show appreciation in many different ways and how that acknowledgment can transform the life of another person. I want this author to speak at our school!!!"

—Victoria Kramer, *Volunteer Room Mom at Silver Spur Elementary School in Rancho Palos Verdes. Mother of two boys, ages 7 and 9*

Yellow Ribbon Week is a program that creates awareness of and action against violence and suicide. Rachel's Challenge is a program urging students to practice compassion and kindness — to motivate, educate and bring positive changes to many young people.

"As you read this book, you will discover that there is true power in The Power of Acknowledgment, through kind actions as well as the spoken word. This book is a living testimonial to the miracles that can occur, and will be life changing for every hand it touches. The passages in this book produce hope through encouraging, uplifting, and motivating words and examples of overcoming life's challenges. The book is written for children, but it totally moved me as an adult and brought me to tears...

I grew up as a military child and I have honorably served military families for many years as a Senior Leader's spouse. Through my experiences I know the *Power of Acknowledgment for Kids* will make a difference in the lives of our nation's heroes and the families of those who serve!! This book has definitely made a difference in my family's life!

Judith, I applaud you and the young contributors to this book for having the courage and strength to share their extraordinary stories. I will definitely use this book in my personal life and with the clients I serve! YOU ARE AWESOME!!!!!"

— Alfrieda Adams, PhD, *Counseling Psychologist and Suicidologist*

You're Totally Awesome!

The **POWER** of Acknowledgment for Kids

Judy Umlas

with a team of FANTASTIC kids

 IIL PUBLISHING, NEW YORK

Published by IIL Publishing, New York a division of International Institute for Learning, Inc. 110 East 59th Street, 31st Fl., New York, NY 10022.

www.iil.com

IIL Publishing books are available at special quantity discounts to use as premiums and sales promotions or for use in school training programs. To contact a representative, please email Vanessa.Innes@iil.com or call 212-515-5177.

Cover and book interior by Maria Scharf Design.

Library of Congress Cataloging-in-Publication Data available.

ISBN 978-0-9708276-7-8

This book is printed on acid-free paper.

Contents

Contributors

Stories in *The Power of Acknowledgment for Kids* were contributed by a fantastic team of young people.

My personal thanks to each of these wonderful kids for working with me on the instructive and engaging stories that follow, which I have only slightly dramatized or added to. I acknowledge each contributor for his or her powerful role in helping to spread the word about the power of acknowledgment to their generation! And what a difference that will make in the world. I know it will have a really positive effect, and for that I am very grateful.

— Judy Umlas

Michael Wagreich

David Wagreich

Dena Salliey

Deja Salliey

Sammy Milhaven

Grace Y. Carter

Jacob Brady

Kaitlyn Emerson

Acknowledgments

Once again I would like to personally acknowledge and thank each of the wonderful young people who worked with me on these amazing stories. I look forward to thanking others as well who will be inspired to contribute their stories through our website, blog and possibly a future edition of this book once they read these! I acknowledge all of them for their powerful participation in helping to spread the word about the power of acknowledgment! Together, we will make a difference and change the world for the better.

I acknowledge my wonderful family, friends, colleagues — and especially President & CEO of International Institute for Learning, Inc., E. LaVerne Johnson — for all of their ongoing belief in this message and their loving support. My special thanks to Associate Publisher Vanessa Innes who helped me bring this and other world-changing books to life, and to Maria Scharf, whose excellent design made this book become utterly readable and fun! And thanks to my editor Stefanie Armstrong, who kept reminding me that I needed to write the great stories the kids told me in "kidspeak."

I dedicate this book to my two-year-old grand-daughter, Lilith Armstrong, who represents possibility, empathy and kindness. She is a real model for what the world can and will be like if we all have something to say about it – which we obviously do!

In short, I think you are all awesome!

In love and light,

Judy Umlas

Author's Note

The Pain of Bullying vs. the Power of Acknowledgment

In my view, acknowledging is as close to the opposite of bullying as you can get! The best thing about acknowledging someone is that it makes others feel good about themselves! Acknowledgment builds confidence and self-esteem, both for the givers and the receivers. The person who gives the acknowledgment ends up showing bravery, because they are willing to do something unusual and point something out that most people take for granted in someone else.

It also feels good to make someone else feel good! This helps to build self-esteem. Bullies, on the other hand, say mean things and make people feel bad because they are scared and feel bad about themselves. They think putting someone else down or hurting their feelings makes themselves powerful and feel like they are in control so they don't have to be afraid of anyone else.

When someone is acknowledged, it makes them feel noticed and appreciated and proud, also building confidence. It gives them the encouragement to achieve more in their lives. It also teaches them how to acknowledge others, thereby spreading the love.

When someone is the victim of bullying, their self-esteem goes way down. They feel alone and ashamed. The world would be a much better place if people pointed out the good instead of the bad in others. Everyone would feel freer to be the best "selves" they could be! (Maybe if someone found out what the bully wasn't being acknowledged for that was making them so angry, and acknowledged them for it, perhaps that would make all the difference in the world.)

So let's try that ... for a change!

Introduction

THERE ONCE WAS A REALLY NICE FAMILY WITH A FEW kids, a dog, a mom and a dad and a grandma who lived with them. One of the kids' aunts, Judy, had written a book for grownups called *The Power of Acknowledgment*. People found that just by reading the book, their lives would change for the better. The word "acknowledgment" that Auntie Judy talked about means this: to tell someone something nice that you notice about them, or how they are special, and not just keep it inside.

"You know, Auntie Judy, Michael is a very good soccer player!"

People at their jobs who read the book started to act much nicer to each other, to have more fun and to get more done. So Auntie Judy was asked to speak to a lot of people about her book. That's why she came to California where Michael, age 7, and David, age 5, lived to give a speech to a group of 1,000 people about it. And, of course, Judy couldn't miss the opportunity to spend some time with her nephews.

"Why are you here, Auntie Judy?" both boys asked. Since Judy and her family live in New York, visits were special and didn't happen very often.

"I am talking to people about my book," she told them.

"What's it called?" they both asked at the same time.

"*The Power of Acknowledgment,*" she said proudly.

"What's acknowledgment?" Michael asked.

"It's something you say to or about a person that makes him or her feel very happy and proud of themselves. It's something nice and it must be true or it's not an acknowledgment!" she added. "Would you like an autographed copy of my book?" she asked them with a smile, thinking they would probably prefer something with cartoons or animals or superheroes.

"Oh yes," they both said together.

Auntie Judy wrote, "Dear Michael and David, You are wonderful nephews and I love you very much!" Then she gave it to them to share.

A little while later, Michael and David were

playing with a big yellow beach ball, throwing it back and forth to each other. Auntie Judy was reading a newspaper.

David said, "You know, Auntie Judy, Michael is a very good soccer player!"

Auntie Judy answered, "That's great!" and told David how proud of him she was for saying something so nice about his brother.

"And that's an ACKNOWLEDGMENT!!!" David shouted with a big smile. Auntie Judy laughed out loud, and thought how nice it was that David got the point so well and so fast. About an hour later, Michael was curled up on a big comfy chair, reading the copy of *The Power of Acknowledgment* that Auntie Judy had just given to him and his brother. She could hardly believe her eyes, and felt very proud of Michael for reading a book for grownups.

A few minutes later, Michael said, "Auntie Judy, you are a really good writer!"

"Thank you" Auntie Judy said, and felt very happy and surprised.

"And THAT was an ACKNOWLEDGMENT!" Michael yelled out.

Auntie Judy laughed so hard that she shook, and realized that this is something that kids could not only understand, but use in their lives, and have fun with, too! That's when she decided to write this book for you guys – all of you who can put it to use from your youngest years to when you are grownups.

So to make it really interesting, we are going to use characters who are based on real children like Michael and David, with real stories that they gave us, but that I have exaggerated or played up just a little bit.

Now let's get started!

Principle #1
Many people deserve acknowledgment!

IT WILL BE EASIER FOR YOU TO ACKNOWLEDGE YOUR friends, parents, teachers, and relatives if you start by practicing on those people you may not know very well. These people are part of your community, and they will be so happy if you show them that you notice what they do and that you care about it. Then you will begin to make the world a happier place!

"I really like the way you are cleaning those windows! You make them sparkle!"

Chapter 1
Getting Started

A Cupcake for Hector

It was a beautiful, sunny California day and Michael was very excited. Tomorrow would be his seventh birthday and he knew that wonderful things were in store for him. He was doing great on his soccer team, loved the sport and was a natural at it. The coach and his proud parents let him know about his growing skills. Michael loved going to school! His first grade teacher made him feel good every time she let him know what a good job he had done on a project, on a spelling test or just on a regular homework assignment. It made him want to try even harder the next time on whatever it was she assigned the class.

After his Mom dropped his five-year-old brother, David, and him off at school, he headed to his class. On the way he saw Hector, the janitor, cleaning some of the classroom windows. He was working very hard at making the glass shine, and Michael just felt like saying hello to him and telling him what a good job he was doing.

"Hi, Mr. Hector!" (The children at his school called every adult Mr. or Miss or Mrs.) Michael nearly shouted his greeting!

"I really like the way you are cleaning those windows! You make them sparkle!"

Hector smiled broadly and thanked Michael for saying such a nice thing to him.

"It makes me feel good to know that you kids actually appreciate what I do!" he said, looking truly happy.

What Michael didn't know was that this smile stayed inside him for the whole day and made him feel "sparkly" himself. In fact, when he got home that night, he went up to his wife who was busy cooking dinner for Hector, herself and their two children.

"Guess what?" Hector said with a big smile.

"What!?" said his wife, smiling back, feeling happy to see Hector smiling. Since Hector sometimes came home looking really tired and sad, this was a very pleasant change for her.

"One of the first graders, Michael, came up to me as I was cleaning the windows and told me how he liked them so sparkly and he actually thanked me for doing this job!" Hector couldn't contain his excitement. "I don't know exactly why," he said thoughtfully, "but this made such a big difference in my day. Most of the time I feel like no one even notices what I do, let alone cares about it. I always feel bad that I didn't stay in school when I was younger," he said sadly. "So if I can make one kid happy with what I do, that really makes me feel like I am making a difference, even in a small way."

The rest of the evening went well – Hector kept Michael's acknowledgment in his heart into the next day and actually came to work with enthusiasm.

What Hector didn't know was that Michael had something else up his sleeve as a way of saying thanks to Hector. Michael knew that his mom was coming to school the next day with cupcakes she had baked for all of the children in his class to celebrate his birthday and for his really nice teacher. On the way home from school the day before his birthday, he told his mother about the great job Mr. Hector had done on the school windows. Edna was pleased – she liked knowing that the school was being kept so clean and "sparkly" and told Michael that it made her happy to hear that.

"Mom," said Michael kind of thoughtfully. "Do you think when you make cupcakes for the kids in my class you could make a special one for Mr. Hector with his name on it? That would be so cool and I think he would like that very, very much."

Somehow Michael knew that his acknowledg-

"It makes me feel good to know that you kids actually appreciate what I do."

— • 7 • —

ment earlier that day had lit Hector up, as if he had turned on a light switch. He had a feeling that this special treat would make him even happier!

"Sure, honey" said his mom. "I would be happy to do that and I think that is very sweet of you to think about someone else who probably doesn't get too many treats at school." There were lots of reasons Michael could hardly wait for the next day!

The next day, Michael jumped out of his Spiderman bed even before Mom came in to wake him up. His brother David was still under his Batman covers fast asleep, but that didn't stop Michael from brushing his teeth and getting dressed, without even waiting for his mom to put his clothes out or asking for breakfast.

"I can hardly wait to get to school," he shouted to everyone in the house, even though each person was in a different room doing his or her own thing.

Grandma Lupita got up, gave Michael a big hug and wished him a very happy birthday. Then Mom, Dad and David – who was finally up due to the shouting that was going on – all hugged and kissed him and wished him a great birthday. His birthday party wouldn't be until the weekend, but he intended to have a spectacular real birthday at school.

After Mom dropped David and Michael off at school, Michael ran to see Hector, who smiled broadly as he came into view.

You are doing an awesome job, Mr. Hector!"

"Hi, Michael!" he nearly shouted.

"Hi, Mr. Hector!" Michael returned with equal enthusiasm.

Today Hector was polishing lockers in the hallway, and they were shining so brightly that Michael could see his own face reflected on the beige surface.

"Wow!!!" Michael exclaimed. "I can see my face on the locker door! You are doing an awesome job, Mr. Hector! And guess what!?"

Hector couldn't help grinning from ear to ear, just from the acknowledgment. And he knew that Michael was about to tell him something very important.

"What?" he said enthusiastically and waited

excitedly for the response.

"Today's my birthday," Michael nearly shouted, "and there are going to be some great treats to celebrate it!"

"That's terrific," Hector exclaimed.

He held out his hand to Michael for a grownup kind of handshake which Michael thought was really cool. They shook hands, said goodbye, and Michael ran off to class.

What he didn't know was that Hector was remembering his own seventh birthday, and how special he had felt when his Mom made him a wonderful chocolate cake. He had felt full of love and happiness. That was before all of the family money troubles had started and he couldn't even get a cake on his next birthday. He continued his cleaning and polishing and still felt great, even with the sad thoughts, because someone had appreciated his good work. He always put himself into whatever he did 100%, but most of the time people either didn't seem to notice or didn't seem to appreciate it. That little guy was sure the exception!

It was two o'clock and Michael was nearly jumping out of his seat with excitement. He knew his mom would be walking in the door any moment now.

Suddenly there she was, with a huge tray of her delicious-looking chocolate cupcakes! She had made them extra special this year. Every child had his or her own name written in either pink icing for girls or blue icing for boys. Sprinkles of every color made them look extra yummy, and Michael's cupcake not only had his name on it, but also a big wax number 7 candle stuck into it. Edna brought the cupcakes to the front of the class, and handed the tray to Mrs. Nelson. The kids couldn't sit in their seats a moment longer as their mouths watered at the sight of these scrumptious treats.

As Mrs. Nelson waved the students up to the front of the class to get their cupcake, they jumped up and gathered around her.

"Let's all wish Michael a happy birthday and sing the song to him. Then we can eat these delicious looking cupcakes," the teacher said with a smile.

Michael, who had jumped up, too, went and whispered something to Mrs. Nelson and his mom. They looked very happy and his teacher told him to go ahead and do what he wanted to do.

The kids all stared as Michael left the classroom. Where was he going? They wanted to sing to him and get started on those cupcakes, which were practically calling their names out loud.

Mrs. Nelson said that Michael had something very important to do and would be right back. She told them to work on their homework assignments until he got back, so they wouldn't have to do them at home!

They all grumbled a bit, but sat down again. A few minutes later Michael came back, holding Hector's hand, and pulling him into the classroom. Hector looked a little confused but that didn't stop Michael.

"Come on, Mr. Hector," he shouted. "Come on, come on!"

The children were gathering around the cupcakes once again. Michael reached up to the tray and found the one with "Mr. Hector" written in beautiful green letters, surrounded by sprinkles. He took one of the little paper plates, put Hector's cupcake on it and handed it proudly to him. Then Michael got swept up into the birthday song being sung by 22 voices, and the glowing candle with the big "7" on it. For a minute, he forgot about Hector.

When the children had each taken the cupcake with their name on it, and sat down to eat it, Michael went over to Hector who was just standing there, holding the cupcake on his little plate.

"Eat it! Eat it!" said Michael.

Then he noticed something that made him a little nervous. He saw a tear trickling down Hector's cheek.

"Are you okay, Mr. Hector?" asked Michael, wondering what could have happened in that short time.

Edna, in the meantime, had noticed the tear as well. She spoke to Hector in Spanish for a minute, since they were both from Mexico. He answered her in Spanish and Edna smiled.

"Michael," she said, "Hector is so happy that you included him in this celebration that he is crying tears of happiness. You did a very good thing, sweetheart and I am very proud of you."

By then, Hector had wiped away the tear and was starting to eat his prized cupcake.

"This is so delicious, Michael. I thank you from the bottom of my heart for including me in this. I never had a cake or a cupcake with my own name on it and it is very, very special."

Michael took the "7" from his cupcake and put it into Hector's cupcake.

"I would like it if you kept this candle, too. That way you can remember this day after you finish the cupcake." And then he ran off with the other kids to play with puzzles and finish out the day. It had been a very, very good birthday.

Questions for kids

Name three kinds of people that you meet in your life that you don't know very well, but who do something special for you. Here are a few examples:

- Your bus driver

- Your mail person

- Your waiter at a restaurant

_____

_____

_____

Tell what these people do that is special. Here are some examples:

- Smiles every time you board the bus, and knows your name.

- Brings your mail right to the door sometimes and greets you nicely.

- Knows your order because you come there a lot, and asks if you want that today.

_____

_____

_____

_____

What could you say or write to that person that would let him or her or even their boss know that they are special and that they are doing a good job? What ways could you say it? By letter? In person? By a telephone call? By texting them on their cell phone? Come up with a creative way of your own.

_____

_____

_____

_____

_____

How do you think you would feel if you acknowledged that person? Describe the feelings in at least five words!

_____

_____

_____

_____

_____

_____

How do you think that person would feel? Describe the feelings in at least five words.

_____

_____

_____

_____

_____

_____

_____

Principle #2

Acknowledgment is a great way to create better and happier relationships with your friends, classmates and family.

ACKNOWLEDGE THE PEOPLE AROUND YOU IN AN honest way. What can you say to your friend, classmate, brother, or sister that lets them know the good things they do? Be prepared for the amazing, positive changes in your friendships and in all of your relationships!

"These are fantastic!"

Chapter 2

Using the Power of
Acknowledgment to Create
Great Friendships and
Get Along Great with
Just About Everyone!

Brandon's World

All the way on the other side of the country, in New Jersey, seven-year-old Deja and five-year-old Dena were talking about school and their favorite teacher, one they had both had in kindergarten. They both loved her so much that they called her "Aunt Janelle" and they also enjoyed names she called them as well over the years. "Super Girl" was Miss Janelle's current name for Dena, who was telling her big sister what fun she had in school.

"I could learn anything from Miss Janelle," Dena said, using the teacher's formal name. "She makes everything so easy and so much fun and I just love to do the 'play-work' she gives us to do at home."

Deja sighed and remembered how much fun

"Super Girl"

she used to have in Janelle's class too, when "homework" was called "play-work." Now it wasn't so much fun, but she did it anyway because she had learned to spend a lot of time on her projects and was now in the habit of doing her assignments 100%, even if they weren't as fun anymore. Back then for Deja, and now for Dena, it always seemed like play – puzzles, drawings, fun things to do that made them proud of themselves. And when their mom saw what they had done, she was always amazed and told them how talented they were. Miss Janelle just made everything so easy!

Today, something was bothering Dena. She was the one whose chubby cheeks made every grownup pinch them and tell her how cute she was. She was pretty tired of that by now, but put up with it cheerfully most of the time. While she and Deja talked about the "good old days" for the older sister, who was actually somewhat jealous of Dena's good luck to have Miss Janelle as her teacher right now, Deja noticed the sad look on Dena's face.

"What's wrong," Deja asked, knowing her little sister well.

She was sure something was bothering her and since they both had been so happy a moment ago talking about their favorite teacher, she was very confused.

"I'm just thinking about how lucky I am," Dena said with a sigh.

"So why is that bugging you?" Deja asked.

"Because Brandon isn't so lucky," she said with a sigh.

"Why, what's going on with Brandon?" Deja asked curiously. If Deja didn't know her little sister better, she would have thought Dena was about to cry. But that just couldn't be...or could it?

Dena looked as if she had a big secret she wasn't supposed to tell. But it suddenly exploded from her.

"Brandon always misbehaves in class," she said sadly, "and Miss Janelle sends him to the back of the room...every day, and I feel like crying every time it happens. It's like Brandon can't help what he is doing, and he still gets punished for it!"

"Wow! That's a tough one, little sister. What does Brandon do that gets the teacher so upset?" Dena was thoughtful for a moment, and then told her sister how her classmate just didn't seem to be able to sit still, and jumped about when others were quietly reading or coloring.

"He makes a lot of noise, as if he is trying to get Miss Janelle's attention all the time. But the only attention she can give him is to yell at him and put him in the back of the room. I just wish I could help him," she finished sadly.

"Well, maybe there is something you can do," said Deja. Dena instantly brightened up.

"What can I do?" she asked excitedly. "I really

want to help, but I'm only five years old, remember?"

"I think Brandon is looking for attention," Deja said wisely. "He needs to know that he is good at some things – he is, isn't he?"

"Hmmm…" said Dena thoughtfully. And then she screamed, "Yes, he draws the best cartoons! I can't believe how good he is at making a real comic strip! He is soooooo good at that, but it's not work, so he doesn't get good grades or gold stars for it."

"Do you tell him how good his cartoons are?" Deja asked her sister.

"Oh, yeah! We all do!"

"All of you tell him how good his cartoons are,

or just the kids?" she asked, sounding like a young lawyer.

"Oh, just the kids. Not Miss Janelle!"

"Well, why doesn't Miss Janelle tell him how good his drawings are then?" wondered Deja.

"She never sees them!" said Dena. "Brandon always hides them whenever Miss Janelle comes close. Instead, he makes a lot of noise, and shoves the pictures into his desk just in time when he gets sent to the back of the room."

"Oh, I get it," said Deja with a smile. She thought about all of this for a minute and then said, "Dena, you have to convince him to show his drawings to Miss Janelle. Are they 'appropriate' for school? You know, the way Mom would say to us?"

"I think so," said Dena. "They are really funny and cute and fun to look at. Sometimes he makes the kind of cartoon that you draw a little bit of on each page and when you flip them, they move – like a kid riding a bicycle! I think they are great!"

"Okay, here's the plan! Are you willing to be a leader and help Miss Janelle help Brandon?"

"Oh yes!" Dena exclaimed. "I want to help!"

"That's my sister!" Deja said proudly and gave her a quick but affectionate hug.

The next day was a Saturday. Following the plan the two girls had worked out, Dena asked her mom if Brandon could come over and play. She knew he lived close by because they rode the school bus in the morning together. He was just at the next stop. Her mom looked surprised by the request, but consulted the class list and decided to give Brandon's mother a call. She had known that Brandon wasn't having an easy time in school and thought it was nice that Dena wanted to reach out to him. Brandon's mom sounded so happy at the invitation – almost relieved.

"I'm sure he would love to play with Dena. He talks about her a lot," she said hopefully. "He tells me how much Miss Janelle loves Dena."

Dena's mom listened and said what she could to reassure her, which was not a lot.

"Tell him to bring his drawing pad and pencils," Dena yelled out.

Plans were made and at exactly twelve o'clock, Brandon appeared full of excitement and smiles.

You have to bring this to school on Monday and show it to Miss Janelle."

After a colorful, artistically-prepared and healthy lunch, Brandon and Dena spent the next two hours drawing cartoons. Deja had stayed around to give a little direction, and to praise Brandon's artwork. Dena's art was another story! By three o'clock, Brandon had created a whole comic strip about his visit to Dena's house, complete with Dena's mom's specially prepared lunch. The result had them all laughing and admiring the work of the little artist.

"You have to bring this to school on Monday and show it to Miss Janelle,"

— • 34 • —

Deja said sounding very sure of herself.

"No, I wouldn't do that," Brandon said sadly.

"Why not? These are fantastic!" Dena cried.

But it was when Deja told him that he had real talent that his face changed. He actually got misty-eyed, and then a big smile broke out on his face.

"Do you really think so?" he asked the older and therefore wiser sister.

Moms always believed their kids had special talents, so they didn't count – neither his nor Dena's mom was a reliable source. But Deja was another story.

"Brandon, I am going to check up on you!" she threatened. "I'm coming to your class on Monday just before the bus comes to take us home, and if you haven't shown those drawings to Miss Janelle, I'm going to tell her about them myself."

He looked both shocked and pleased to be threatened about something he cared so much for.

"Well, okay…" he mumbled. He was really, really scared. But he was very excited as well.

Monday came too fast, and while the students were trickling in, Brandon swooped by Miss Janelle's desk, dropped the drawing pad on it and ran to the back of the room, where he was often sent for misbehaving. Not knowing what he had dropped off but looking rather suspicious, Miss Janelle walked toward her desk and opened the drawing pad. She looked over the three pages of cartoon panels slowly, and as she did so, her jaw dropped. Brandon, who was facing the rear wall, did not see her expression but did hear her loud voice.

"Brandon, could you come to my desk please?" she said so that everyone could hear her.

Now she didn't usually start scolding him until all of the students were in the circle and he was starting to act out. This was pretty unusual. He turned around, terrified, but then witnessed a true miracle. Miss Janelle was looking at him with a big – no, it was really a huge – smile on her face.

"Brandon," she said in amazement, flipping the pad back to the first page of drawings. "You are a very talented young man! I would like to put your cartoons on the bulletin board so that everyone can see them. You even wrote the words in the cartoons so beautifully. Did someone help you?" she asked.

"No, but Dena's sister checked my spelling and helped me fix a few mistakes," he admitted.

"Well, that's great!" she said in acknowledgment. "In fact, what you have done is so good that I am wondering if you could do a cartoon about things that happen in our class. We could have a contest and see who can come up with the best name for the series," she said, getting carried away by idea after idea for making the cartoons somehow a part of the kindergarten lessons or beyond.

The next day, everyone wrote down their ideas

for the title of the cartoon series, with a little help, and Miss Janelle read each one. Each child voted for the one he or she liked best and "Brandon's World" won by far. That was the one Brandon himself voted for, even though it had been Dena who created it. It was great to have a friend like Dena, one with a big sister like Deja.

And an interesting thing happened that day, even though Miss Janelle didn't realize it until school was out. For the first time in weeks, Brandon did not act out in circle time. In fact, he just kept paying attention and smiling, as if he had some happy secret inside him. And he did.

Questions for kids

Think of someone you know in school that people may have trouble dealing with. What could you find to acknowledge about that child? Think hard, because sometimes you have to imagine more than what you see to find the good. Here are some examples:

- He or she is a great athlete, even if they don't make friends easily.

- He or she sings beautifully.

- He or she can tell a joke better than anyone.

Think of what happened to Brandon after he was acknowledged by his teacher. How did his behavior change?

_____

_____

_____

_____

_____

What role can or should a teacher play in acknowledging the students?

_____

_____

_____

_____

_____

_____

_____

Make up a different end to the story of Brandon, one in which Deja and Dena didn't convince him to show his drawings to his teacher. Tell how Brandon is at age 7, age 10 and age 12.

_____

_____

_____

_____

_____

_____

Name three people you know who could do well from your acknowledgment of them and of how special they are in some way:

- a friend

- a family member

- a classmate or teacher

_____

_____

_____

_____

_____

Principle #3

Acknowledgment makes jealousy go away and helps create a better friendship, even with a person you may not like very much.

IF YOU SAY SOMETHING NICE TO AND ABOUT THE person you are jealous of, you can watch how your feelings of jealousy go away as they try to share their special talents with you!

"Since you're so good at acting and singing, do you think maybe you could help me so that I could try out too?"

Chapter 3
Using Acknowledgment to Take Away Jealous Feelings

Lights, Camera, Acknowledgment!

Their success with Dena's friend Brandon made both girls feel really great and proud of the good deed they had done. They were starting to realize that they could do some pretty fantastic things together when they weren't arguing. Their mom had been telling them that for years, but until they saw Brandon's success because they worked together on this "project," they hadn't really believed her. All moms think that, and tell their kids that, but was it really true? It seemed that something good had happened and they knew there was more where that came from.

But now something else was bothering Dena. It had started small, but it was getting bigger and bigger. Last year, Deja had been in not one, but two school plays: *The Music Man* and *Twelfth*

Night. That had meant a lot of rehearsals that Dena was dragged along to, especially when the show was getting closer. The students had to rehearse after school and even a couple of evenings. Oh, it was so boring to hear those lines over and over again, and to hear the music from *The Music Man*. Dena did like the songs though, and even found herself singing "76 Trombones" when she didn't even know she was doing it. That "Pick a Little, Talk a Little" song really got to her – it was a fun one. Now Deja had a pretty good part – not the starring role – but she was Zaneeta, the mayor's daughter who did some fun and sneaky things and who got to sing the fun song "Shipoopi!"

Dena knew all the words of the songs by now –

she had to come to rehearsals often enough. But she didn't get to do anything with how much she knew! All she could do was watch, and she knew she could not only sing but could dance as well. She imagined herself as Marian, the town librarian who had a really big part. Oh, she could sing those songs really loud all right, if anyone would just ask her to.

And then in the spring, Deja found herself in *Twelfth Night*, a play by that guy who didn't even know how to talk so people could understand him, William Shakespeare, or something like that. And Deja, her big sister, was Sir Andrew – a boy! How could that be? Oh, how she hated the long, drawn-out rehearsals that she got dragged to as the date of the play got closer. She would never want to be in a play like that one. Not her! Give her a part in a musical and she would be happy, but not that ridiculous character that Deja played (except maybe when he was in a duel with Cesario, that part was pretty cool). Deja sure made her laugh when she said her lines – she really made Sir Andrew sound like a weirdo, which she guessed he was supposed to be. And she was sure she could do the dueling part. Oh well…it just wasn't fair. There weren't any big plays like those at her school. But next year… well, she wasn't going to think about that. It was too much work, and their mom made her go to all three nights of each of the plays. It wasn't fair! It wasn't fair… And Deja got tons of flowers, too, for both her roles in both plays. That was really not fair. She thought that she should be getting flowers just for coming to all of those rehearsals and performances!

Whenever she complained about it to Deja, her big sister got a little smile on her face and said in her "I'm bigger and better than you" voice, "You're just jealous!" and Dena went and sulked by herself in her room. It wasn't even worth an answer, she thought.

Finally, the plays were over for the year and she could just look forward to having a great summer. Then in the fall, she would think about going to her new school – the same one that Deja went to. That could be pretty cool, except if everyone wanted her to "act" like Deja. Then she would be in trouble.

Before she knew it, it was September and school had started. It was scary going to a much bigger school, with kids from all over the area and all different ages, and bigger too. But after a few weeks, she knew her way around, loved her new teacher and had made some good friends. Brandon was still in her class, and he seemed to be doing really well. Their new teacher seemed to know from the beginning how good at cartooning and art he was, and he already had the job of helping Ms. Frankel create a weekly newsletter about their class activities! That was awesome.

Then one day, it happened. An announcement was made over the loudspeaker that try-outs were being held for the next school play. It was *The Sound of Music* – one she already knew and loved because she had seen the movie with Julie Andrews in it about a thousand times. She had asked for the movie as a holiday present the last year and had gotten it, so she already knew a lot of the lines. Deja came home and told their mom that she was trying out for the big part of Maria. She wanted to at least try, even though she didn't think she could sing all of those high notes.

"That's wonderful," her mom told her. "You should certainly try, and even if you don't get that part, I'm sure you will get another really good one."

Dena started to boil inside – that's what it felt like. "What about me?" she wanted to yell out. "I could sing and dance and I already know a lot of lines in the play! What about me???" But instead of saying anything out loud, she went to her room and stayed there for a long time.

Finally, her mom called her out to do homework and get ready for dinner.

"What's wrong, Dena?" she asked. "You look upset."

"Well, yeah," Dena blurted out. "I could be in that play too if I tried out!"

"So why don't you? I think that would be great!" her mom assured her.

"No," she cried, tears welling up. "I can't do that – only Deja can be in those school plays! She's so good at them!" she wailed.

Just then, Deja came into the kitchen where Dena and her mom were standing.

"What's going on?" she asked curiously. Their mother started to explain, but Dena interrupted her and just jumped in with everything that was on her mind. She couldn't hold it in any longer!

"Deja, you are so good at acting and singing and dancing, and you always get good parts in the school plays and I am so jealous of you. Everyone pays attention to you, you get the flowers, you act like you're the star...which sometimes you are...and I feel so left out. I don't know if I could do as great a job as you do, but I'm too scared to try out. So there! Now you know what's bugging me!" she cried out and stamped her foot for empha-

"Deja, you are so good at acting and singing and dancing..."

sis. Then, a new thought seem to cross her mind.

"Hey, wait a minute. Since you're so good at acting and singing, do you think maybe you could help me so that I could try out too? I would be so scared, but maybe if you helped me…"

Deja was quiet for a minute and then looked affectionately at Dena.

"Well, you sure did put a lot of time into rehearsals for the plays last year even though you weren't in them. You definitely should get credit for that. And I know you know a lot of the lines from *The Sound of Music*. Why don't we pick a part that we both agree you would be good at, and then I'll work with you to get ready for the audition," she said with warmth.

"What's an 'addition'?" Dena asked.

"AU-dition," said Deja. "It's a try-out, and I can help you get ready for it if you are willing to work really hard."

Dena was stunned. For a moment, she just thought about what Deja had offered and was completely quiet.

Then she yelled out, "I want to be one of the Von Trapp children who sings!"

"I'm sure we could get you ready for one of those parts," assured her big sister.

The next day, the two sisters met up after school to hear about try-outs. Each was given a song and written lines to practice. As soon as they got home on the late bus, Dena was ready to start. Deja smiled with pride at her little sister's excitement, and they didn't come out of their room until dinner time. They played parts of the video of the musical at least five times! Try-outs were not until the next week, so they started to practice, practice, practice each day as soon as they got home from school. Their mother could hear their voices getting stronger and stronger. Anyone walking by their living room could see how much fun they were having.

Finally, the big day – auditions for *The Sound of Music* – came. Deja was nervous; Dena was terrified, but they went in to the auditorium together and to all of the other kids, and even to the teachers, the girls looked totally confident. It was clear that both girls had practiced a lot and had the willingness to work hard for what they wanted. They knew the audition lines, knew the songs, sang in key, and weren't shy about their volume. The teachers in charge nodded to each other, showing they were impressed, as each girl tried out.

On the way home, Dena said to Deja, "Thanks for helping me. I didn't do too badly, did I?" Deja got a big smile on her face.

"You did great, little sister! You made me proud!"

The next day, there was a list of people who would be in the play. There had only been a few parts for the youngest children, and Dena's name was on top of that list! Deja had not gotten the part of Maria, but she had been chosen to be

Liesl, the sixteen-year-old daughter – which was also a huge part! Both girls screamed when they saw their names and jumped up and down in excitement, hugging each other.

Dena thought about what a huge help her big sister had been in her getting such a great part. She knew she could have stayed jealous and mad, but it had worked much better to tell Deja how jealous she had been of her great success, and ask for her help. What a great reward that created – for both of them. She could really see that now.

On opening night, many guests – both family and friends – showed up, with loads of acknowledgments for the great job each girl had done! And both got bouquets of gorgeous flowers this time.

Questions for kids

Think of someone you know in school that does something better, maybe even much better, than you. It could be playing a sport, writing stories, getting math problems right without studying, or anything else. Think of how you feel when you see their skill or talent, and you don't have that one. Which applies to you?

☐ I wish I had that talent, but I wouldn't tell him/her that!

☐ I will just pretend I don't see how good he/she is at _____.

☐ I like that talent and feel jealous of him/her, but I'm willing to tell them and ask for their help or coaching.

Write your feelings and what actions you are willing to take.

_____

_____

_____

What did it take for Dena to tell Deja she was jealous and ask for her help?

☐ She felt so jealous that it made her angry.

☐ She just ignored the situation and hoped it would be better this year.

☐ She knew she had to take some action or else she would have to pay the price of watching her sister be in more plays which would make her more jealous.

What role should your parent or parents take in this kind of situation: is it better to let it be worked out between you and your sister, brother or friend, or for your parent to get involved?

_____

_____

_____

_____

_____

_____

Make up a different end to the story of Dena's jealousy, one in which she doesn't ask Deja to help her and just stays jealous. Tell how Dena deals with all of Deja's plays in the coming years.

_____

_____

_____

_____

_____

_____

Name two people you know that you are jealous of that you could acknowledge, and maybe get to "coach" you in their talent or skill. It could be:

- a friend

- a family member

- a classmate or teacher

- other

_____

_____

_____

Describe what it is that you are jealous of, and what you could say to that person. Write your own "script" with what you say, followed by what they say.

_____

_____

_____

_____

_____

_____

Principle #4

Being acknowledged for good things leads to great feelings and terrific results. Not being acknowledged for good work makes you feel angry and sad.

BEING ACKNOWLEDGED FOR BEING A GREAT PERSON OR DOING A GREAT JOB MAKES people feel encouraged, happy and also makes them want to be even greater or do even more. If someone works really hard at something and no one tells them what a good job they did, they wonder if it was worth doing.

Chapter 4

How Acknowledgment Helps You Do a Great Job in School and in Your Extracurricular Activities

Making a Difference – Jennifer's Story

Jennifer was a good kid. She tried pretty hard at school, and wanted to do well. She was generally liked by her classmates and friends. She was one of those kids who never got into trouble, usually turned in her homework on time, studied for tests and got pretty good grades, but never got particularly noticed for anything, either good or bad. Sometimes she felt like she was invisible.

She had so many ideas in her head, that sometimes it just drove her crazy. And she never told people about them – not even her best friend, Allison. For example, every time she heard about a global disaster on the news – a hurricane, a tornado, a tsunami, and then saw the way people were affected – she imagined herself getting on a plane and going there. She got a very clear vision of boarding the plane, getting off in the middle of the disaster and just rolling up her sleeves and helping – for as long as it took to help bring things back to normal.

And the "picture" she would get in her mind could be anywhere! She wanted to help, but in a big way, an important way. She wanted to bring medicines to foreign countries where people were sick, or get food, clothing and water to people that needed the supplies. She would always send part of her allowance and babysitting money to the Red Cross or UNICEF or some other organization that went to where the problems were. But she was too shy to tell her friends or classmates, or even a teacher what she would really like to do – and that was to help people in ways that really made a difference.

The only person she could even hint at this stuff with was her Grandma. Her Grammy, Jann, was a really cool lady whose job it was to help put together conferences for teachers and coaches and others who helped people. She would help bring in speakers that would make them feel better about themselves and make them be more able to work with and really help other people, like kids, for example.

The truth was, Grammy was really her best friend because she knew how much she was loved by her and how Grammy would never do anything to hurt her. So Grammy had tried to explain to Jennifer what these conferences were about, but they didn't make too much sense. She really just enjoyed going for walks or shopping or going to restaurants with her – when it could be just the two of them.

Sadly, all Jennifer could do was hint at what she wanted to do someday, even with this person she trusted most in the world. Any time Grammy tried to get her to tell her more about her ideas, she just got quiet or changed the subject. She was actually afraid of how real the "pictures" in her mind were. Did that mean she was supposed to do something about them? They were a mystery to her.

Because Jennifer was so good at hiding in the background, she was often terrified that her classmates would call her a "Goody Goody" or "Goody Two Shoes" behind her back if she started really helping people at the scene of a disaster.

That had happened once when she was very little. There had been a story in the newspaper that her kindergarten teacher had read to the class about a family that didn't have enough to eat after a tornado destroyed their home. The teacher said the class could raise some money or bring in some supplies for the family if they wanted to, and she would make sure they got to the address that was given in the newspaper. The article gave details: there were six kids and the mother was really sick with some disease Jennifer couldn't even pronounce, and the father was trying to rebuild their house. Jennifer's heart had hurt when she heard about this family.

She went home after school that day, went

straight to her room and just cried. Her mom asked her what was wrong and she told her about the family that needed so much money and clothes and food. She told her mom she wanted to help by giving this family her whole penny collection that was in a huge jar that she had been saving up for two years.

Her mom said that would be okay. So with her mom's help, she brought the jar that was about half as tall as she was, to school. But that day her teacher was out sick, so the money was turned in to a secretary at the principal's office, who just nodded when she received the jar, and Jennifer never found out if it got to the family. Some kids in her class found out about what she had done, and just laughed at her for giving away all of her own money to people she didn't even know. She felt embarrassed, sad and hopeless.

Eight years later, she was still upset about this whenever she thought about it. Two things about what had happened hurt her a lot: the first was that she had never been appreciated or acknowledged for her generous donation, and the second was that she never found out if it got to the family and if all of her long-saved pennies had helped even a little bit.

After this disaster, she made a promise to herself that her most important job now was to blend in and not stand out. She didn't want her classmates to think she was foolish, and what little she could do didn't really matter anyway. And besides, she knew she couldn't get to any of those faraway places when storms or hurricanes struck. It was just some stupid dream or fantasy, like Cinderella or Spiderman or Batman. So she really did a great job of blending into the background.

Whenever she heard about a tornado or a hurricane she might have thought about helping out at, she thought about her jar full of money and just felt hopeless and sad. Over time, she stopped putting out a big effort for just about everything. Her grades got worse. She didn't always bother to hand in her assignments on time. She didn't feel too good about herself by now. She had even stopped helping her little brother Dennis with his homework and projects when he asked her for help. She felt like she was a "lump on the couch," as she confided to her friend Allison.

Then one day, just after her 13th birthday, her Grammy gave her a special invitation: to come and help out at one of the big conferences she was organizing. There were going to be about 1,000 people at this one, people with many different jobs coming from all over the world. But they were all going to be there to learn how to be the best people they could be and help many thousands of other people, including kids, be the best that they could be.

Something moved inside Jennifer when she heard about it – it felt like just some faint little unreachable tickle in her heart, but she found herself thinking about the invitation from her Grammy a lot over the next few days. It would mean flying from Oregon, where her family lived, all the way to Florida! That, by itself, made it something to consider. She had only been on a plane once before when she was very little. It would be such fun to travel with Grammy, too! They would have to share a hotel room together, and it seemed like such a grown up thing to do.

So finally, with her parents' permission, she agreed to go, not having any idea what to expect, even though Grammy tried to tell her. Finally, she decided that she was going to go there for the adventure, and to miss two days of school, which made it worthwhile.

It was her first plane ride since she was very little, and who better to take it with than her Grammy! She was so excited that she got to have a window seat. The plane noises got so loud just before it was about to take off. Jennifer's stomach was doing flip flops in excitement. Suddenly the plane started going super-fast on the runway, and she felt like she was now being pulled, like a magnet, into the back of her seat. She didn't even realize the moment they left the ground until everything out the window got smaller and smaller, like that movie, *Honey, I Shrunk the Kids!* She was so glad she had decided to go on this trip!

When they got to the conference in warm, beautiful, sunny Florida, she was immediately given a printed name tag in plastic, with her name in big black letters. It made her feel very important. Then she was told to do about a thousand things – put out fliers at each seat before the people came, welcome them when they arrived, help them all find seats, show them where the bathrooms were, where to get food, and where they could use their cell phones. She was told to remind them to turn off their phones during the event. She even helped out when people wanted to register for other courses. It was fun and exciting to use the credit card machines.

Wow! She worked like crazy for the three days – it seemed like she never stopped. And she brought water and juice to people like Grammy who were responsible for everything at the conference. Grammy should have had roller skates, she moved around so much.

Jennifer felt like everyone trusted her, even though she was the youngest one there, and wanted her help and also appreciated it. So many people thanked her, told her what a great smile she had, let her know how great it was for a student to help out and give her time. The nice words and actions made her smile almost constantly. While she was helping out, she also found herself listening to the speakers.

There was one lady who spoke about *The Power of Acknowledgment*, and how important it was to let people know how much they meant to you and how important they were to the group or company or school they were working in. She really paid attention to that one, and even thought back to the incident that took place with the pennies, when she was a child, and how NOT being acknowledged for her caring actions had made

"I'm here because my Grammy knew that helping people was something very important to me."

her afraid to help or stand out and make a difference, even though she never stopped dreaming about doing it.

And then, almost before she knew it, the event was ending. The CEO (that was a new term for her, but she had quickly figured out that he was the "Big Boss" – the Chief Executive Officer) came up on the stage and thanked all of the speakers, and all of the people who had come to the conference. He told them that being there would make a big difference in the world, because they would pass on what they learned to others.

And then he did something Jennifer would never, ever forget for the rest of her life. He called all of the volunteers up to the stage, and thanked each of them one by one for being there and helping to make a difference. He had each person tell their name and why they had come.

When her turn came, Jennifer felt like she was going to faint. But then she stepped forward and said, "I'm here because my Grammy is my best friend, and she knew that helping people was something very important to me, even though I never really told her it was. She works here and invited me to come. And I'm really glad I did!"

Then applause broke out for her – maybe it was because she was the last person to come forward, the youngest, or maybe it was because people thought she was really great. Whatever it was, she felt very special after that acknowledgment, and she had a smile on her face that went from ear to ear.

Somehow, she knew life would never be the same after this special event. She knew now, without a doubt, that what made her feel happy and full of love was making a difference in as many people's lives as possible.

And this, she knew, was just the beginning.

Questions for kids

Can you remember a time when you did something really special for someone and no one acknowledged or appreciated you for doing that deed? Describe the action in detail. How did you feel when you did it? How did you feel when no one noticed or said anything nice about what you did, and what "decisions" did you make about helping others after that?

_____

_____

_____

_____

If Jennifer's contribution of all of her pennies had been acknowledged by her principal, her teacher and the family that received the contribution, what difference do you think this would have made to Jennifer?

a . No difference.

b . She might have wanted to do some more things to help others.

c . She would have stopped wanting to help people.

d . She would have asked her Grandma to help her organize big events and money raisers to help people.

Should people need to be acknowledged for doing good things that help others, or should they just feel good in themselves for doing good things?

a . They should always be acknowledged, no matter how big or small their contri-bution.

b . They should feel great all on their own, just for doing something to help others.

c . Both would be great!

How do you think Jennifer's life changed after her big acknowledgment at the conference? Talk about:

- her grades

- her need to blend in and not be noticed

- her interests in and out of school

_____

_____

_____

What would you like to do that you are not doing because you are afraid to really stand out or be seen as a "goody two shoes?" List at least three things you would do if you weren't afraid and if you knew all of your actions would be acknowledged and appreciated:

_____

_____

_____

Principle #5

Well-deserved acknowledgments always make a big difference in your life and schoolwork and in the lives of those you acknowledge.

YOU WILL SOON SEE A POSITIVE DIFFERENCE IN YOUR life and schoolwork when you begin to acknowledge others for the help that they give you, and the good jobs they do. Your grades will even improve! And so might theirs.

Chapter 5

How Acknowledgment
Makes a Big Difference in
Your Life and Schoolwork

A "Chipper"
Acknowledgment!

Grace and her dad had just moved to a new neighborhood. Everything felt strange to them both. There was no favorite Chinese food take-out place, no pizza delivery where she knew the delivery boy who smiled at her each time he came over with what she had ordered. Worst of all, though, she had no friends to hang out with.

Why did they have to move – again? It seemed like they moved every two or three years! How was she ever going to get through eighth grade, Grace wondered. She really missed her best friend, Amanda. They had been friends for what seemed to be forever and knew each other's moods, upsets, parents' weirdnesses, their own dreams and wishes, and their most secret sensitivities. Without thinking, they could recite each other's favorite movies and the dialogue from the best scenes. They even knew each other's crushes' birthdays!

To start over was a real bummer. She'd probably be in college before she had a best friend again. The one thing she was happy about leaving, though, was math and her yucky math teacher. He made everything so complicated that she had just about given up entirely on the subject. She had been almost failing algebra. Maybe things would be different – maybe even a little better – in her new school with a new teacher. At least it wasn't hopeless – yet!

The first week at the new school went easier

and better than Grace had expected. The kids were pretty friendly. One girl, Nikki, had even invited her to come over on Saturday to "hang" with a few friends. She lived near Grace, so Grace asked her dad if it would be okay and if he could drive her over there. He was happy for her and said "Of course!" and the girls had a great time.

But meanwhile, the math nightmare continued. The new math teacher was a lot nicer, but he made just as little sense to her. He was also kind of cute, so she paid even less attention to what he was trying to teach. A brand new school, new kids, and new teachers were bad enough. UGH!!! But she was now once again failing math after the first test and quiz. And the quickly done homework (more accurately called "guesswork") earned her a bunch of 60's. Double UGH!!!

In spite of this, she went to Nikki's house pretty regularly on Saturdays and always had a great time. Nikki was so nice. And her other girlfriends were just as nice. Now that was good luck. Grace knew that girls her age could be really nasty and cruel.

But the math teacher, Mr. Sanderson, wasn't giving up on her, even with her poor results in math. He was NOT forgetting about her the way Mr. Jellen had. Mr. Sanderson had actually called (G-r-r-r-r!) to speak to her dad the other night, and Grace had picked up the phone.

"Hi, is this Grace?" a friendly voice had asked.

"Yes it is," she answered, wondering who could

be calling and knowing who she was, without her recognizing him.

"This is Mr. Sanderson!" he said in a friendly way. "Your math teacher," he added when there was silence. "Is your dad around? I wanted to talk to him about how things are going in math class. I think he might be able to help."

(I don't think so, Grace thought to herself. Her dad was too busy solving life's problems, dealing with a divorce, doing his accounting work.)

"Oh, okay," she responded after a while. "I'll go get him." She was tempted to come back and tell her teacher that her dad wasn't home and would never be home again, but instead she got her father from the kitchen.

"Dad, it's Mr. Sanderson, my math teacher," she said in a stage whisper.

"Uh oh?" asked her dad with a half-smile.

"I think so," Grace said seriously, pretty scared.

After a few minutes, Grace's father came back to the family room. He looked kind of sad, but then perked up as he started speaking.

"You know, Mr. Sanderson is really nice and he thinks you can do the work. He just thinks you need some tutoring to catch up, and then you will be able to keep up very nicely. He was pretty encouraging! Like it's not hopeless," he smiled at last.

"But I don't want a tutor, Dad. You know we can't pay for one now. That's one of the reasons we had to move, because we couldn't afford to stay in our old house. Maybe I can just drop Regents Algebra and take just plain old math," she said grimly.

"No, honey," said her father with conviction. He looked thoughtful for a minute and then said, "You are right about the money situation, and tutors can be expensive. BUT...," he said kind of proudly, "I used to be a whiz at algebra." I even made some extra money in college, tutoring other students in math. I think I could handle one as pretty and smart as my own daughter!"

Grace thought about it for a minute, gritted her teeth and said, "Okay, when do we start?"

"How about right now?" her dad said, not missing a beat. Grace grumbled a little and went for her math book and notebook, and they began. They agreed they would do the homework assignments together every night and see where Grace's problems were, and then spend an extra 15 to 30 minutes going over the rough spots.

"Ugh!" Grace said to herself when they finally agreed. Then she said it out loud to her dad.

"UGH!!!" she shouted to him.

"Double UGH!!!" he shouted back, laughing, and then they got down to business.

Almost needless to say, with her dad's help, Grace got all 100's on her homework over the next week. But that didn't mean she was going to pass any of her tests or quizzes. Well, she didn't "pass" – she aced them all! She got in the 90's on the two quizzes that week, and got a 93 on the test the following week. Wow! She couldn't believe how easy it was when she was actually paid attention in her tutoring sessions.

Mr. Sanderson took quick note of the situation. About two weeks after the "tutoring" started, he called again.

"Hi, is this Grace?" he said when she answered the phone.

"Yes, it is! Hi, Mr. Sanderson," she almost sang.

"Hey, Grace. I'm calling this time to congratulate you AND your father. You make a fantastic team, and the results are incredible."

"You can tell him that," she said as she ran for her father.

"Dad, Dad, it's Mr. Sanderson!" she nearly screamed.

Her dad took the phone with anticipation this time. He knew Grace really understood the math now, and had seen the grades she had been taking home as well.

He came back from the call, grinning ear to ear.

"Great job, Gracie!" he said enthusiastically. "Mr. Sanderson says you really are getting your math. Not only that," her dad said proudly, "he said you are going to be one of the best math students in your grade! He said he can tell by how quickly you have caught on to everything!"

Grace looked shocked. She had never considered herself good in math at all. English yes, languages yes, math no. Well, this was one time she didn't mind being wrong.

"Thanks, Daddy," Grace said, getting a little teary. "I'm not going to pay you for helping me, 'cause that's like your job! But I really appreciate how easy you've made it for me to understand stuff that seemed really too hard for me. You have actually helped me change the way I think about math now. It's pretty cool stuff!" she said with pleasure, and scampered off to tell Nikki the news.

Grace's father took a moment to think about what this success had meant to him. He realized that working with Gracie on her math had been like watering

"He said you are going to be one of the best math students in your grade!"

— • 103 • —

a sprout, sheltering it from a big wind as it grew until it was strong enough to weather any storm. Nothing, he realized, was better than doing that for your kid.

Gracie's acknowledgment – letting him know that their work together had actually changed the way she saw math – made him realize the difference he made in his daughter's life and he knew he would treasure her words forever.

Grace's success in math continued. After a while, she and her dad agreed that they didn't need to go over the homework assignments together anymore. She felt a little sad about that, but also proud. She promised to ask him for help if things got rough again, even on something small.

A few weeks later, surprisingly, Nikki broke a

date they had to go to a movie on Saturday. She called Grace to say that she had been grounded, due to not turning in math homework that had been due.

"Wow!" said Grace. "What happened?"

"I guess I'm just stupid, Gracie," Nikki moaned. "I just don't get it. I feel like an idiot."

"Hey, Nikki, I felt the same way until my father had to start tutoring me and I caught up pretty fast. I didn't like doing it, but it really helped!"

"Well my mom and dad didn't go to college – they didn't even finish high school – so I know they can't help me with algebra. And we can't afford some fancy tutor, either."

Grace got a big smile on her face and said, "I

can't believe I'm saying this, but I could tutor you!" And she knew it was true.

"Oh, I don't think I can learn this stuff, especially from a friend," Nikki whined.

"Let's try it," Grace said in her most persuasive voice. "I will get my father to call your parents and tell them how tutoring helped me, and that way they will un-ground you! I'll come over later and we can start. Maybe it won't be as much fun as going to the movies, but I'll make popcorn and bring it with me!"

"Okay," Nikki said a bit uncertainly. "Tell your father to call my parents."

And so Grace started tutoring her friend in math, paying the good deed her father had done for her forward — to her appreciative friend.

Grace showed her ways to do the harder problems in an easier way, and gave her new problems to do to make sure she understood them.

Before long, Nikki was also getting 90's. She was so happy with the results that it seemed to make everything at school seem better than it had ever been. She stopped being so angry at her parents and blaming them for their little bit of schooling. She knew she could lead the way for her family now, and be a student they would all be proud of.

She thanked Grace from the bottom of her heart, and tried to find the best way to show her how much she had been helped. She felt so happy and proud of her success that, with Grace's father's permission and money she had earned

babysitting, she bought her friend a cheerful, chirpy canary. She knew her friend had wanted a pet forever, but had not yet had one because of all of the family's moves and changes.

On the day Grace came over to give Nikki her last tutoring session, Nikki presented her with a gorgeous, happy, chirping canary in a brass cage.

"This bird is supposed to remind you of how happy you made me by helping me become good in math! Every time you hear this bird sing, I want you to think of what you did for me!" she smiled, as the bird, who Grace had already named "Chipper," began to sing.

No other acknowledgment from a friend could have meant as much to her, and it was likely that Chipper would never let her forget about it.

Questions for kids

Can you remember a time when a friend, relative, classmate, or teacher made a big difference in your life? In three to four sentences, write down what that person did for you.

_____

_____

_____

_____

_____

_____

Can you remember a time when you did something to help someone, which in a big way changed their lives for the better? Examples:

- Helped a classmate or friend with their homework

- Defended a classmate or friend when he or she was being bullied

- Befriended the new person at school

Write down how each situation would make you feel. How would you feel if you were thanked or acknowledged for making a difference in someone's life?

_____

_____

_____

_____

_____

_____

Write an acknowledgment of someone who has had a big and positive effect on your life. Be specific as to who they are, what they did for you or how what they did affected you.

_____

_____

_____

_____

_____

_____

Principle #6

For both the giver and receiver, acknowledgment can improve one's health.

ACKNOWLEDGING OTHERS AND BEING ACKNOWLEDGED will help to get rid of stress and bad feelings. This will improve your health, and make you want to work harder to be the healthiest you can be.

Chapter 6

Using the Power of
Acknowledgment to
Be Healthier

Good Enough
Can Be Great!

Eight-year-old Annie knew there was something wrong. She was a third grader who had some really good friends in the neighborhood she lived in. This was the first year she was getting invited to sleepovers, and it was really an exciting idea. But she couldn't say yes, even though her mom and dad had said it would be okay. She was terrified of sleeping over at anyone's house, except her grandma's. She had done that a while ago, and the "awful thing" had happened. She woke up in a wet bed.

Her grandma was someone who knew how special she was (she always told her that), and loved her completely. So when she came into Annie's room in the morning and found her crying, she just hugged her and told her not to worry about what had happened. Children stopped bed wetting at different times, and she would probably outgrow it soon. It was just between them, unless Annie wanted to tell her parents, and that was okay, too.

But Annie's parents already knew about it, because it happened at home at least a few times a week. And then she got the invitation to sleep over that meant the most to her – her friend Nancy said it would be such fun, and two other girls would be there also. They would have a sleepover party, and Annie knew they would be talking about it – or her – for days after.

She couldn't bear it anymore. She told them she couldn't make it because her parents had said she wasn't old enough yet, and then she marched into dinner that night with a purpose, even with her younger brother Johnny there. "Take me to the doctor!" she said to her parents very loudly.

"Why?" asked her mother, with concern.

"Because it's not right for an eight year old to wet her bed."

"Yeah, I don't wet mine anymore," chimed in five-year-old Johnny, and Annie wanted to smack him. Her dad, a pharmacist, thought about it and said to her mother, "Janet, I think we should listen to Annie. I know a very good doctor we can take her to." Both of her parents looked worried, but Annie felt better.

Two days later, Annie and her mom went on the train from Eastchester, where they lived, to

New York City. It was a fun trip, even though Annie was nervous. What would the doctor tell them?

She just knew something was wrong, but didn't know what it could be. But she felt proud of being brave enough to get her parents to have it checked out, and maybe not have to miss other sleepovers. They got to Dr. Pane's office and had to wait such a long time! Finally, a nurse came into the waiting room and called them in. The doctor spoke to Annie and her mother, and then told her she would need to leave a "urine sample" in a cup. Yuck! That sounded pretty gross to Annie. She hoped no one would drink it afterwards by mistake!

Once she had left the sample in the cup (that

was not so easy to do and she missed a bit), the doctor came back to the room she was in. He had put the sample into a test tube, and said he was going to drop a tablet into it. If the tablet turned the urine blue and it stayed blue, that meant everything was okay and they would still look for some way to help Annie with her problem. If it turned yellow, orange or brown (the worst, he said), then they would have to do some things and there would be big changes in Annie's life.

Annie was scared; in fact, she was terrified, as Dr. Pane held the tablet dramatically over the test tube. What was going to happen? What did all of this mean? Then he let it go, and the clear yellowish liquid in the test tube turned a deep and beautiful blue! Annie was so relieved, and didn't even know why. But then right before her eyes, the blue started to change color and became slightly green. And then the green turned to a yellowish color, then a bright orange and at last, the ugly brown that, without knowing why, she so dreaded.

Dr. Pane looked at her mother, not at Annie. "She has juvenile diabetes," he said sadly. "I'm really sorry. We will need to start her on insulin injections right away." Immediately, a nurse came in holding a syringe with a long needle sticking out from it.

Annie started to cry, then scream, then wail, and tried to run out of the room (she always dreaded penicillin shots, or vaccinations of any kind, and gave any nurse who tried to give one to her a really hard time). Finally, the nurse got her in a hold that locked her to her, and jabbed her arm with the needle. Oh, it hurt so much. But if that could stop the bed wetting (could it?), maybe it wouldn't be so bad, now that it was over.

Then suddenly, Daddy was in the room with them – why wasn't he at work? "Peter," the doctor said (he and Daddy knew each other from before), "you are going to have to learn how to give Annie her daily insulin shots. It takes some practice, but you have some medical background and it shouldn't be a problem."

Then Annie saw that Mommy was crying, and Daddy looked pretty miserable. What was going on here? And was she imagining that the doctor had said she would have to take these shots every day? What kind of a mean sickness was that? She would rather keep wetting her bed. Why had she insisted that they take her to the doctor's in the first place?

Mommy cried all the way home on the train, and Annie tried to comfort her. But it didn't help. And when they got home, Daddy tried to explain what diabetes was, and that his father had it but that he got it as a grownup. Annie had another kind of diabetes, just for kids!

"Oh wow! What fun!" she thought sarcastically. She was angry at herself, at her grandpa because maybe he started it, at her brother for not having it, and at her parents for listening to her and taking her to the doctor. Daddy tried to make it easier by telling her that he would give her some coins every day for every shot and she could keep them.

That didn't help at all, and just made her madder. Then she learned more that she didn't want to know. She couldn't have sweets anymore, except if the medicine made the sugar in her blood go too low and she needed something sugary to make it go back up. No more birthday cake, cookies, or ice cream as a snack after school. And what would she eat at friends' parties? She cried for a long time. Her grandma came over and hugged her, which helped a little, but not enough.

Then at school the next day, when things just couldn't get worse, they did. Mommy had driven her to school (usually she went on a bus), and she spoke to Annie's teacher before the class began.

Once her mother had left, Mrs. King, whom Annie really loved, said she had an announcement to make. Then she cleared her throat and said that Annie had developed a sickness that wasn't catching, but that everyone had to make sure she didn't faint or pass out from the medicine she was taking. That she was taking shots every day now, because she had a sickness called diabetes and that everyone, of course, wished her the best.

Annie started to cry, and jumped out of her seat to run to the girls' room. "Wait, Annie," said Mrs. King. "You will be okay after you get used to it. Now please smile and then you can go to the girls' room!" Annie thought she would pass out – not from the medicine in her shot this morning, but from the embarrassment and the 26 pairs of eyes on her, with some laughing and snickering in the background. She created a fake, horrible, twisted smile – one that she would never forget the pain of – and ran out of the classroom.

Weeks went by, and every month she had to visit Dr. Pane. He would make her leave a "sample" and was never happy with it. He always told her mother that Annie was not doing well, that she must be sneaking sweets or there would not be so much sugar in her urine. And then the nurse would give her an extra shot for that day.

Wasn't it bad enough to have to get the one that Daddy had to give her? That one hurt, it was embarrassing, and her Daddy seemed pretty miserable about it, too, but tried to act cheerful. Her mom told her that maybe one day it would

get better and all go away, but then Daddy would take her mother aside and they would argue in a whisper. "You know it won't go away – until they find a cure," he would say angrily. "Don't give her false hope!" he hissed, and Annie would hear them.

In the meantime, her cookie stash was getting low (she had found a box of Oreo cookies, and some candy bars in the back of a kitchen closet before everything was thrown out). She was so upset after going to the doctor, and he would yell at her, that she would go into her room and steal from her stash. Why should she be "good" when the doctor was so mean to her?

Then one day, she saw him drawing red dots

on her chart, after he had examined her eyes. "What are those dots?" she asked the doctor. "Oh, nothing," he said. "But please makes sure you are not eating any sweets or there will be problems. "What kind of problems?" she asked, scared. "Big ones," he said and that was the end of the conversation.

Every month a magazine called *Forecast* would come to the house about diabetes and kids. Annie's mother would grab it, read it and then pass it on to Annie, who started to notice that a few pages were usually ripped out of it. "What did you take out of *Forecast*?" Annie asked one day.

"A recipe," her mother said.

"Oh," Annie responded and flipped through the articles, most of which were very boring.

Then one day, she got home from school before her mother was home, used her key, and then got the mail from the mailbox. There was *Forecast* and she decided to flip through it. "The Unavoidable Complications of Juvenile Diabetes," it announced in a big headline. The list made Annie burst into tears: blindness, kidney failure, amputations of arms and toes and legs. And the list went on. She shrieked in pain, and stayed in her room until dinnertime. And then she screamed at her parents, "Why didn't you tell me about this?" And they both looked ashamed and heartbroken. "We didn't want to upset you any more than you already were," they said. Mommy was crying again. Daddy looked like he was about to.

From then on, things got worse, not better.

Any chance she got, Annie ate what she knew she shouldn't, especially after seeing Dr. Pane who continued to yell at her and tell her she was going to one day have to "pay the piper." She hated him, and dreaded going to see him. It was years later that she learned that the red dots were the beginning of the complications of diabetes in her eyes. She sensed it was something bad, but he wouldn't tell her.

Then one day, her parents decided to take her to another doctor for her checkup. She didn't know why, but she would have done anything to avoid Dr. Pane, so she didn't object too strongly when her parents told her that it was instead of going to see that awful man. The new doctor's name was Dr. Zickle, which rhymed with "tickle" and almost made her smile.

First he had her come into his private office just by herself. That was a little scary, but also made her feel grown up. "Annie," he said and smiled at her. "I know you have been through a lot. Diabetes is not a lot of fun. It's hard work, the shots are a pain in the neck or wherever you get them," he joked "and you have to give up a lot of things you love. But we can be in this together, if you want me to be your doctor. And I told your parents that it is really up to you. A lot of people in my family have diabetes, and that's why I became a doctor that treats children as well as adults with it. I really do know how hard it is. Even my sister has it!"

"Really?" Annie said, very surprised. She immediately liked this doctor 100 times better. He didn't seem to be against her – she felt he was on her side.

That day she went home, and threw out the secret candy stash she had kept growing whenever she was at a party. She didn't feel like she needed it so much. And she could have a "treat" once in a while, even with her parents' knowing, according to the new doctor.

The next visit showed a big improvement. The tablet turned only green, instead of turning orange and brown, and Annie knew that she had allowed the insulin to work better this time, although it still wasn't perfect. Instead of getting mad at her or telling her she should try harder, Dr. Zickle got a big smile and said, "I'm so proud of you, Annie. I know you are really trying and there isn't anything more I could ask of you!"

"What about asking me to make the tablet turn blue instead of green?" she asked, a little scared of his answer.

"No, Annie! You are really trying, and it's impossible to be perfect. Good is good enough!" Then she gathered up her courage and asked him about all of the terrible things she had read and his answer helped.

"If you do a good enough job, which you are doing," he said with a warm smile, "those things probably won't happen to you. Just do the best you can, and sometimes you will need a little break. And that's okay with me."

Annie left in a happy mood for the first time

ever after seeing a diabetes doctor. Dr. Zickle had made the difference to her. He had acknowledged her for her efforts. He believed that she was trying and she only wanted to do better and better for him, for her parents and most of all, for herself!

(Author's note: Many years later, "Annie" received an award from a diabetes research center called the Joslin Diabetes Center, for "living courageously with diabetes for more than 50 years," and for accomplishing this without any of the complications of the disease, a testimonial to her "good enough," if not perfect, blood sugar control, promoted by the great model for Dr. Zickle, Dr. Donald Zwickler. And in these times, there are many treatment advances, if not yet a cure, that make control for diabetic children much easier than it was.)

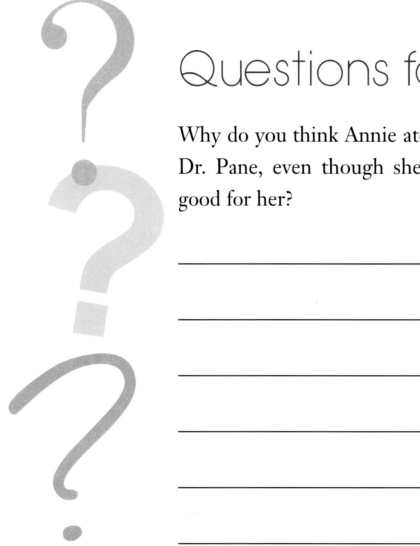

Questions for kids

Why do you think Annie ate sweets after seeing Dr. Pane, even though she knew they weren't good for her?

_____

_____

_____

_____

_____

How did Dr. Pane make things worse by telling Annie that she would one day have to "pay the piper"? What does this mean to you?

_____

_____

_____

_____

_____

_____

How do you think you would you feel if a doctor or nurse told you something bad would happen to you if you didn't do what you were told (like lose weight, gain weight, go to bed early, etc.)? Did that ever happen to you and if so, how did you behave?

_____

_____

_____

_____

_____

_____

Do you think all medical students who are becoming doctors or nurses should be taught the importance of and how to acknowledge their patients, and if so, why?

_____

_____

_____

_____

_____

_____

Why was Dr. Zickle so successful in helping Annie feel better about herself and in getting healthier?

_____

_____

_____

_____

_____

_____

The Healing Power of Acknowledgment

J acob loved the summertime. He got to do all of the things he enjoyed: swimming, boating, playing tennis, and just having a great time. He also loved being able to visit his good friend Max, whose family had a summer place in Rhode Island. For the past few years, Max had been inviting Jacob to come with his family to spend a few days, because they used to be best friends when they both lived in New York City, but Jacob's family had moved and it was harder to stay in touch. And Jacob's parents had thought he was still too young for the trip so far away from home and family. But this year, when Jacob turned 12, he was allowed to stay at Max's house for five days! During that time, they would have the chance to catch up on everything they couldn't manage to keep up with on Facebook, daily texting on cell phones and even an occasional (though pretty rare) actual telephone call!

At last summer was here, and Jacob was counting the days until he could leave for Max's house. Max's house was right near the water – his family owned a boat that had a powerful engine, and they would go water skiing, tubing and swimming for hours on end with them. Even though

Max wasn't a big daredevil and Jacob was, they still always had fun together.

At last the long-awaited day finally arrived, and Jacob's family took him to the city to meet up with Max's family. They made the four-hour trip to Rhode Island, but the time in the car flew by. Jacob knew it would be almost constant water fun for him and Max – that's what they loved most to do, and Max's mother always had a portable refrigerator filled with great food so they would be able to picnic and stay out a long time when they went out on the boat. They spent a fun and quiet evening in the summer cottage, and Jacob had a great time exploring. He had heard Max talk about the cottage and the beach for years, and Jacob had always been so eager to come along.

Now the chance was here!

The next day, Max's parents took the boys to a water park, where they had fun on water slides, going tubing down some chutes (actually Max sat that one out – he was a bit less courageous than his pal) and just having fun.

The day after that was a perfect day for boating – sunny, clear, just a few puffy clouds in the sky. Jacob and Max always had so much fun together – once on the boat, they began horsing around with boat ties and ropes, and just playing. The family had a large tube on the boat, even though Max didn't want to use it. But Jacob "signed right up" for that ride. He loved adventures, and had never gone tubing in the ocean or any large body of water before. He was a strong swimmer, so no one was overly concerned when he fell off the tube after a brief run in with the tube being pulled by the boat. Max's father, Miles, slowed down and pulled up next to him. His dad kept the motor running as he neared Jacob.

It only took a split second. A split second that would change a life, a family, the world as Jacob knew it. It was just a split second of not thinking the "rescue" operation through. It was something that could have happened to anyone. But disaster struck, and struck hard. Immediately, the propeller of the boat started pulling Jacob in by his legs. What Miles didn't realize – until he heard the screams – was that the propellers had gotten tangled with Jacob's legs. Jacob, meanwhile, wasn't even sure what was happening. He was scared and hurt and suddenly the awful truth hit him – he knew that he could no longer swim. His legs, which he had felt were being pulled or almost sucked into the propellers, suddenly started to feel as if they were being pushed away. Jacob didn't know what that meant, but he felt that he was being almost lifted by some force away from the harmful propellers. When he started to sink into the cool blue waters – the scene until a moment ago of such fun and joy – Max's mom jumped in the water to get him and used lifesaving techniques she hadn't needed since the course she had taken when she was a teenager. With Max's dad's help, they managed to get Jacob out of the water and onto the deck of the boat.

Miles immediately called 911 for an ambulance

to be there for them at the dock. Max, meanwhile, was devastated at how badly hurt his best friend was, and went down below in the boat crying and sobbing, himself. He couldn't take the sight of his friend being in so much pain!

Jacob desperately wanted his friend to go with him in the ambulance – what an adventure that would have been if one of them was not so badly hurt. But Max just couldn't summon up the courage and calmness that were necessary and instead, his mom came and held Jacob's hand. But he was getting more and more terrified. "I don't want to die! I don't want to die!" he shouted over and over. He begged Max's mom, Beth, to call his mom and dad, which she did.

The ambulance rushed Jacob to the nearest

hospital, a tiny one in comparison to any New York City hospital, but Max's mom kept saying, "You're going to be okay. I promise!" By this time, IV fluids were dripping into Jacob, he was getting woozy and the pain already seemed less.

Meanwhile, Jacob's mom and dad had just gotten the awful news back in New York. Before the phone call was even over, the two – who had been at a local beach having a nice afternoon – were organizing a trip to Rhode Island, calling a baby sitter and running for their car. Jacob's mom and dad, Mr. and Mrs. Brady, begged the doctor in Rhode Island to wait until they arrived to start the surgery, but they were told that this would be too great a risk. This couldn't wait – surgery was necessary, complicated and needed to be done right now. Reluctantly, the shocked parents gave their permission and started praying.

Jacob was terrified. He had never had surgery before – he had not even had stitches or a broken bone in his twelve years. But before he knew it, he was being wheeled into a glaring white and brilliantly lit operating theater. *House* and *Grey's Anatomy* had done a pretty good job of preparing him for how it would look, but not for the shock and panic he felt. This couldn't be happening!

Three hours later, he awoke to his parents' concerned and anxious faces peering over him. He could barely make them out, he was still so groggy, but somehow it made things seem better just to have them there. Then he started to feel the pain of the accident and the surgery. The anesthesia was wearing off. He had never experienced pain like this in his life and hoped he never would again. Although his parents wanted to take him to a New York hospital right away, a raging fever kept Jacob in the Rhode Island intensive care unit, with his mom and dad sleeping by his bedside for a week. Max's mom, devastated by the turn of events, came every day with presents for Jacob and iced coffee for his mother. Each one knew how awful the other must feel, and tried to do their best to make things better.

One week later, Jacob was transferred to a children's hospital closer to home. His mom rode with him in the ambulance this time, because he was really nervous. His dad followed them all the way in the car. Nothing about the experience was easy – Jacob spent seven more weeks in the New York hospital, with three more surgeries. As brave as he tried to be, he was deeply frustrated, angry and sad. He could no longer walk, and had a really hard time even keeping his food down. The need for medicines of every size, shape, taste and drip was a constant. He was hooked up to machines, including a wound vac which was attached to both of his legs. He had never even heard of such sophisticated equipment, not even on any of the medical TV shows.

The days were very long, and even with his family around, Jacob seemed to be losing his spirit, his fun and mischievous sense of humor, and even his desire to make the necessary comeback. It was just too hard.

At around this time, many people heard about his accident. Friends, relatives, teachers, storekeepers, camp counselors, religious leaders and principals who knew Jacob and cared a lot about him started sending cards, balloons and snacks. Then people started emailing him. He began to really look forward to letters and emails. It meant people were thinking about him, and that meant a lot. They knew his situation was beyond challenging – it was nothing any 12-year-old boy, or anyone, should ever have to endure. People knew that they needed to acknowledge Jacob for who he was and the contribution he made to all of them. His aunt and uncle sent him a PlayStation and a laptop to help fill his time, and the laptop made it possible for people all over the globe to reach out to him via email and instant message to let him know how much he mattered to them. He heard from kids and teachers from his old school, as well as the new middle school he had been attending. Brownies from one of the assistant principals made a huge difference to him.

So many people wanted to show they cared. A friend of his parents called the Mets, who then sent Jacob a get well package, which included a signed baseball and a baseball hat! Some friends contacted World Wrestling Entertainment on behalf of Jacob, who was one of their biggest fans, and they sent him a framed WrestleMania XXVI aerial print and three shirts! His dad's friend, Jack, sent him a life-size cutout of his favorite wrestler, John Cena! A friend of the family knew he liked the singer Chris Daughtry, so they asked him to make a video get well message for Jacob, which he was happy to do.

Imagine! All of this was truly awesome, and Jacob took it in and got a real-pick up when he was feeling down, when he was maybe at his lowest point.

The endless acknowledgments went on and on. People just wouldn't tolerate Jacob not knowing how much he was cared about. His grandparents came to visit him every chance they could. His best friend, Reed, did too. He would try to make Jacob laugh, and then take silly, funny pictures with his cell phone, which made him laugh harder. Then he would post the pictures on Facebook and many of Jacob's friends would respond with jokes and cheerful greetings and encouragement. He also got a teddy bear from the people at his new school. The two Rabbis from his synagogue visited too. One blew the shofar, a kind of trumpet used during one of the holidays that Jacob was missing. Jacob was seeing first-hand how much he mattered to people. But still, it was a huge challenge to keep working at regaining the skills like walking and even moving his legs that had come so easily to him before.

Jacob's sister Emily knew she had to do some special things for him to make sure he knew how much she cared about him and his recovery. Even though they had fought a lot before, she now insisted on sleeping in the hospital with Jacob and their mother.

It was finally time to come home, but the journey was far from over. He came into the house he had not seen in months in a wheelchair, and had to sleep on a hospital bed in the living room.

A year later, Jacob is walking but cannot go to school full time yet. His wounds are still healing, and he needs consistent physical therapy. His suffering continues, but his spirit is stronger than ever. He now knows fully – in his heart of hearts – the difference he makes to people. All of those friends, family members and even perfect strangers who acknowledged Jacob made him feel stronger than the trauma of his injuries and the demanding care that followed.

Those people helped him get to the place he is today – ready to accept any challenge – by letting him know how much he mattered. His ever loyal friend Reed said recently that he was starting to see "the old Jacob" again – with all of his spunk and at least some of his mischief. In fact, at Reed's Bar Mitzvah, Jacob stood up to acknowledge his friend for his ongoing love and wonderful support. In a very un-13-year-old way, and with just a little embarrassment, he gave Reed a big hug in front of about 200 friends and relatives, and said to him, "You are a good 'man,' Reed!" – taking note of the ceremonial transition to manhood that the Bar Mitzvah represented. Tears and laughter swept through the synagogue, and Reed was happy that Jacob was able to have people see his fun-loving spirit returning. He was also deeply appreciative of the acknowledgment – it had been a long and a rough haul, but one he never would have wanted to avoid. Just being there for his friend was his gift both to Jacob and to himself.

Later, Jacob remembered very clearly how big a difference it had made to him when people sent him WrestleMania sheets and Spiderman blankets and other colorful brands of bedding and room decorations while he was in the hospital. Kids from other rooms on the floor used to come in just to see his hospital living space – it was so UNLIKE a hospital. As a result of this, he decided to take on the project of collecting SpongeBob,

Disney Princess, Hannah Montana, Spiderman, Batman and other cheerful pillows and blankets for children's rooms throughout the hospital, and has been delivering them ever since.

What a relief – for all of the people that knew and loved him – to have the real Jacob back. And without a doubt it was the power of acknowledgment of Jacob, by so many people who cared, and for Jacob, who then found his own ways to acknowledge others – that has allowed this both miraculous and challenging recovery to take place!

Now fully recovered, Jacob thought of how he could pass along the wonderful feelings he experienced as a result of being acknowledged by so many people. Like a light bulb, an idea flashed in his mind, and Jacob knew exactly what to do. He would show his appreciation for others. As his mind filled with images of all the people he wanted to acknowledge, he kept coming back to his parents. They had always done everything to take good care of him, but now especially, he couldn't forget their huge concern and worried expressions when he was hurt. He always knew his parents loved and cared about him, but at this instant, Jacob realized how much this had meant to him since the accident. He wasn't sure if he had ever told them that, and now Jacob was determined to change that. He didn't want to just text them (his usual form of communication). He wanted to do something special. With a pencil in hand and a piece of paper, Jacob set to the difficult task of writing them a personal letter of acknowledgment.

It took a few tries for the words on the page to come out right, but Jacob filled with pride as he folded his written acknowledgment and slid it into an envelope. He sealed the envelope, put a stamp he had found in the family 'junk drawer', and with a big grin, he walked outside to the mailbox on the corner. He put the envelope inside for the post office to mail back to his parents. He couldn't wait for them to read the first of many acknowledgments to come. And maybe even that mischievous sister of his deserved one, too…

Questions for kids

Did you ever know anyone who had a really bad accident or illness, and who needed support from family, friends, teachers and others? If so, who was it?

_____

_____

_____

_____

What did you do to help in this situation? What could you have done to make the person feel like they mattered, like people made Jacob realize he did? What could you have said to acknowledge that person?

_____

_____

_____

_____

_____

_____

How does making someone feel that they matter improve their health and well-being?

_____

_____

_____

_____

_____

_____

_____

What can you say to a sick or injured friend to
make them know that you care about them?

_____

_____

_____

_____

_____

_____

_____

Who would you acknowledge if they were seriously hurt?

_____

_____

_____

_____

Would you still acknowledge that person if they weren't hurt?

_____

_____

_____

Principle #7

There are many different ways to acknowledge the people in your life who deserve it, and to show your appreciation.

YOU CAN SHOW YOUR APPRECIATION to a friend, a family member, a teacher, a principal, or a coach in many different ways. Acknowledge them by writing them a note, drawing a picture, telling a teacher what a good job a classmate did on a project. A coach, a parent or a teacher can also acknowledge you in many creative and wonderful ways.

Chapter 7
Practice Many Different Ways of Acknowledging People!

Blood, Sweat, Tears...
and Cheers!

*C*laire could tell you what playing basket-ball meant to her in three simple words – what it had always meant, since fourth grade: BS&T or Blood, Sweat and Tears. It represented her day-to-day experiences on the basketball court – on courts in 23 states, in big schools and small ones. Her team played in cities from Los Angeles to New York, where the kids had tried their hardest to win, and often did. BS&T stood for the words that meant success to Claire and to her team-mates. Since she was nine, she had been putting those words into action on the basketball courts.

Claire was following a tradition – one she was very proud of. Her dad, George, one of five kids, had played basketball nearly 24 hours a day, 7 days a week when he was her age. He loved most sports, but basketball was his passion. As one of five kids, he didn't stand out much on the family "team," but sports were another story. He played sports all over New Jersey, where he was the star of the local teams.

George was a star in basketball. And it felt good to be the star. And suddenly, he was "picked up" by a Division One college – where the sports teams were the best, and where his team won and won, and won again. His coach was so tough that George thought he would fall apart at times. The yelling and screaming cut right through him, and even made him want to quit at times.

But even taking everything his coach shouted at him to heart, George just didn't get the play time he wanted. Sometimes he went in as a sub and made some big headlines in the sports sections of the newspapers. He helped his team win the National Invitation Tournament or NIT. But his journey took him far from home in order to get the playing time he knew he needed: it took him to Ireland, where he actually had ended up playing on a pro team for two years. What an experience!

Claire loved hearing stories about those days. She couldn't imagine going so far from home to get the playing time she wanted and needed so badly. But when she reached sixth grade, Coach Pete brought her down. Practices were tough, with a lot of running and drills. And it was her first real traveling team. What made it even worse was that she was the youngest on the team, playing with older kids. All of the other girls on her team were more advanced than she was in the game.

Though she wasn't the best, she always gave it a full 100% effort. Now, she was used to tough coaches in fourth and fifth grade, but the toughest coach – at least on her – was her Dad. He loved the job, he loved the game, but needed to make sure no other parent accused him of playing favorites with his kids. So he came down even harder on them. It was a tradition he was used to anyway – all of his coaches had been shouters and screamers. Sometimes he wondered why the kids took it at all! But he knew it had worked for him as an athlete and felt it was his job to pass this on to all of the kids, especially his own, who had a natural talent for the game, and many possibilities for success ahead of them.

He also knew that this magical game would keep them away from drugs and alcohol, and teach them how to help their teammates, show appreciation for others and play on a team the way they would need to do later in life in the business world.

Over time, George had learned that it took a lot of energy for a coach to be so negative with the kids – to keep up the constant yelling. He was learning with his third child that positive comments were a big help and decided to try it out in getting the best out of his team. He found it took a lot less energy to acknowledge the good stuff than to scream out against the bad. He had learned to tell them that maybe the move wasn't right, but here's something they DID do right. And they just seemed to eat it up and perform better and better. Wow! What a discovery!

It was painful for George to see Claire's coach using the traditional, negative tactics he had grown up with. He was a witness to how it deflated, de-energized, angered and upset the kids. Why do it this way?!

Claire was winning the games but losing her drive and her love for the game. Although Coach Pete guaranteed her playing time – a big deal for a ninth grader – she had been brought close to tears many times by his everyday yelling and screaming.

He would criticize almost everything she did; whenever she made an honest mistake, he would take her out and yell non-stop at her. Tears were the natural and miserable result for Claire. And when she did something great, he would never applaud her. A simple high-five for doing something well would have been a miracle. She wasn't asking to be praised for a layup – she had been doing that successfully since fourth grade! Her confidence was now ruined, and she started doing something she had never wanted to do or had to do before: complaining to her parents. She even told them she didn't want to play anymore – her father's worst fear!

Coach Pete made her simply not want to play the game. He took away the fun and her love of basketball. She began dreading practices, knowing she would be yelled at, and was actually scared of games. It was a true nightmare for her.

Her parents finally gave her the option of either quitting the team or finishing it out – it was her choice. Even her father recognized that the coach had just gone too far. But Claire did not see herself as a quitter, and chose to stick it out to the end of the season.

The truly sad part was that Claire, who had always had such confidence when it came to basketball, was now constantly second guessing herself, and was absolutely terrified of making a mistake. She was so scared of Coach Pete yelling at her.

Later in the season, things came to a terrible and dramatic head. Coach Pete had a daughter on the team named Laura. While she was a nice enough kid, she was not too skilled in the sport. At every game, Coach Pete and his daughter ended up screaming at each other! Imagine! It was shocking and uncomfortable for all of the other parents, and certainly for the other kids on the team.

Almost every game was an unimaginable screaming match, and none of the other girls on the team got coached in any of the important ways they needed. At their last game, the coach actually got down on his knees – not to pray, for sure, but to scream at all of the girls at the top of his lungs, even using curse words that no kids – let alone their parents –wanted or needed to hear. He actually shouted and cursed at the girls, while screaming and jumping up and down!

At that, the referee, who had been watching the action closely, stopped the game, and made the coach leave the school and go out to the parking lot. It was over – but the game was really only now just beginning.

After that, Claire and her team had a new coach – one who recognized her accomplishments, along with those of the other girls. It took a while for all of their confidence to come back, but it eventually did. Their new coach, Coach Franklin, rewarded the girls for achieving their goals in basketball. They learned that making a bad move was just part of a bad day, rather than being a life-defining moment. The next game could be their great one and the coach made sure to reward their hard work not only with praise but with hugs!

During a game, one of the players made a basket, but accidentally scored for the other team – the worst play imaginable. It was clear that Claire's teammate was about to break down in tears, as soon as she realized her mistake. That had to be the most embarrassing moment of all in a player's life.

But Coach Franklin started clapping instead of screaming, and soon the parents followed his lead and stood up and cheered the player, who ended up laughing instead of crying. Coach Franklin had led the way, and the team felt the power not only to be great, but to make mistakes without being killed for them. And that only added to their desire to win and make their wonderful coach as proud as he could be.

Claire finally knew and recognized the power of acknowledgment to make the game rewarding and fun, as did every member of her team.

Questions for kids

How would you feel if you were not acknowledged for your great efforts in sports? Write down three words describing your feelings.

_____

_____

_____

How can a coach acknowledge his or her players?

_____

_____

_____

How was Claire's basketball game improved after Coach Franklin joined the team?

_____

_____

_____

Why did Coach Franklin decide to applaud the player who accidentally scored for the other team? How did this make the situation better?

_____

_____

_____

What were the positive effects of the team as a whole when they were acknowledged? Compare it with the negative effects they received when they were yelled at, or just not acknowledged.

_____

_____

_____

_____

_____

_____

You're Totally Awesome!

In closing...

You have read the amazing stories about acknowledgment from our fantastic team of kids. Now International Institute for Learning wants to invite you to tell us YOUR story about your experience of The Power of Acknowledgment – or the lack of it.

We may even ask you if we can publish what you write on our blog or in a new book! And we encourage you to illustrate your story!

Please write to me at: **judy.umlas@iil.com**! I really want to hear from you!

And remember,
"YOU'RE TOTALLY AWESOME!"

Hugs to you all,

Judy

You're Totally Awesome!

Judy Umlas is the author of three books, and she is also an International Institute for Learning, Inc. (IIL) trainer and Senior Vice President (www.iil.com).

Her books include:

The Power of Acknowledgment
©2006, IIL Publishing

Grateful Leadership - Using the Power of Acknowledgment to Engage All Your People

Judy has worked at IIL for 20 years, following a career in television at CBS and then at PBS. Her work with *The Power of Acknowledgment* and *Grateful Leadership* is Judy's personal passion and her mission. She travels around the world training people in all kinds of businesses. She intends to keep getting this message out until the whole world makes a change for the better!

Notes

You're Totally Awesome!

You're Totally Awesome!

Notes

You're Totally Awesome!